VIVA PONCHO

twenty ponchos & capelets to knit

christina stork · leslie barbazette

STC CRAFT | A MELANIE FALICK BOOK | NEW YORK

Published in 2005
STC Craft: A Melanie Falick Book
115 West 18th Street
New York, NY 10011
www.abramsbooks.com

Canadian Distribution:
Canadian Manda Group
One Atlantic Avenue, Suite 105
Toronto, Ontario M6K 3E7
Canada

Library of Congress Cataloging-in-Publication Data

Stork, Christina.
  Viva poncho : twenty ponchos and capelets to
knit / Christina Stork & Leslie Barbazette.
    p. cm.
  Includes index.
  ISBN 1-58479-421-6 (pbk.)
    1. Knitting—Patterns. 2. Cloaks. 3. Shawls. I.
Barbazette, Leslie. II. Title.
  TT825.S754 2005
  746.43'2043—dc22   200459136

Designed by Leslie Barbazette

The text of this book was composed in Interstate

Printed in China

10 9 8 7 6 5 4 3 2 1
First Printing

Stewart, Tabori & Chang is a subsidiary of
LA MARTINIÈRE

contents

credits & thanks

WE'D LIKE TO THANK OUR

Photographer
David Verba

Editors
Marisa Bulzone, Melanie Falick, Dee Neer,
and the folks at Stewart, Tabori & Chang

Knitters
Lisa Morter, Matthew Sumner, Sonya Philip,
Rachael Herron, Marilyn Stemerick, Jennifer
Hughes, Keiran Best, Tessa O'Donnell, Amy Hsu,
and Michael Baum

Models
Christina Lozano, Lisa Solomon, Rachel Konte,
Assata Konte, Jonathan Hunt, Hiya Swanhuyser,
Keiran Best, Amy Hsu, and Brigid Hewitt

Symbolcraft Creatrix
Dee Neer

Thanks to the customers and staff of Article Pract
for being such a source of inspiration.

Thanks to our families and friends for making
us the strong and sassy ladies we are today.

introduction

Sick of scarves? Have you knit one too many hats? Eager to try your hand at a garment, but want something a bit more accessible than a sweater? You're not alone.

We think ponchos and capelets are a perfect "next step" for a newer knitter and a welcome break for old hands. Ponchos are also great teaching tools: they take the knitter step-by-step through techniques that can seem daunting if attempted all at once.

One of the things we love most about ponchos is their flexibility. There are many basic shapes and within each shape are myriad possibilities. You can easily take a basic shape, add your favorite design elements, and make it your own. On the following pages you'll find basic shapes, to which we've added some details to create 20 different ponchos and capelets. You'll see all the tools we used to create our versions—you can either play with ours or create your own.

history

Variations on capes and capelets have been worn for centuries. Consider, for example, the *paenula,* a hooded, circular cloak made of wool or leather that was worn by the ancient Romans. Or the *huque,* a short, flowing tunic with open sides that clothed medieval Europe. The poncho has its roots in the *serape,* a heavy, woven horse blanket worn like a shawl or sewn together in traditional Mexican and Navajo cultures. But it wasn't until the mid-1960s that the poncho became a fashion icon.

It was during that time that American politics and cultural attitudes manifested themselves in fashion by rebuffing some of the more formal and coiffed ideals of the past. Ponchos, caftans, Nehru jackets, and other garments from "foreign" traditions were embraced by the hippie culture as statements of global consciousness.

As the 1970s approached, the craft movement took hold of fashion, first by way of tie-dye and batik, and then by means of all forms of handmade clothing.

As punk and New Wave moved in, ponchos and hippie fashions moved out—and onto the children's racks in clothing stores. Most of us who grew up in the 70s had a poncho—Christina liked to wear hers backward over her head, pretending she had long hair.

Now ponchos are back in fashion, big time. We're seeing them across the board—on the runway and at the mall, on moms, tweens, and babies too. And why not? Ponchos are the perfect accessory: they're easy to wear, can be dressy or casual, and are just right for a chilly night at the beach or the over-airconditioned office.

That's why we say "Viva Poncho!"

how to use this book

Each project needs the right tools, and the poncho is no exception. We need the right yarn—and the right needle to get the correct gauge with that yarn. But we'd like to offer you more tools to play with: design tools.

Each section of this book is concerned with a different type of poncho: one-piece, two-piece, and capelet. Within each section

you'll find more options: squares, raglans, circles, cardigans—each design element gives you the opportunity to select the look and shape that's most appealing to you.

Then the tools get refined once more: Do you want to add a stitch design to your garment to give it that special look? Perhaps you'd rather use more than one color, or a variegated yarn to achieve your vision?

Then there are the little touches, what we call "add-ons." These tools allow you to complete the picture in style. Feel like sporting a cowl neck or a hood? We'll teach you how.

Here's our very simple formula for achieving exactly what you want in a poncho or capelet:

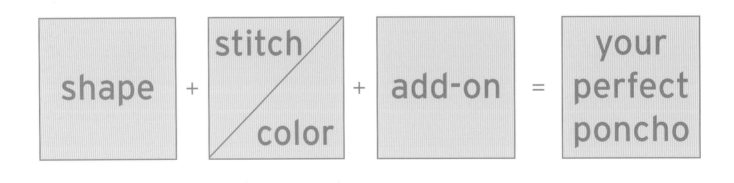

shape + stitch / color + add-on = your perfect poncho

Amelia *and* Frida *are examples of how to customize your poncho using a stitch pattern.*

Mae *and* Greta *are examples of how to customize your poncho by changing color and choosing add-ons.*

Each section represents a different shape. Look at all the patterns to get a sense of types of ponchos.

Ginger *takes on a new appearance with yarns of different colors and textures.*

skills chart

We know that not every knitter learns the same way, and not every knitter has the same set of skills. To find out which ponchos might match your skill level, check out our handy-dandy skill chart on the opposite page.

The chart will tell you all the skills needed to make each poncho in this book—and which skills you'll be learning. This way, you can grow your skills while you grow your wardrobe by knitting through the patterns in this book.

SKILLS NEEDED	PATTERN	SKILLS LEARNED
cast on, bind off	Sonya, page 66	stockinette stitch
knit	Tessa, page 56	increase and decrease, garter stitch
stockinette stitch, increase and decrease	Carson, page 28	pick up stitches
knit and purl, pick up stitches	Sanchez, page 24	seed stitch, single cast-on method
knit and purl	Duchess, page 114	rib, make one increase
rib	Amelia, page 74	use a repeating stitch pattern
stockinette stitch	Monte, page 96	turn your work (short rows)
garter stitch, decrease	Eloise, page 92	yarn over
yarn over, garter stitch	Gilda, page 50	drop stitches on purpose
yarn over, decrease	Mash, page 42	alternative cast on: knit-on
yarn over, decrease	Desirée, page 46	add fringe
knit-on cast on, stockinette stitch	Mae, page 70	change color, weave in ends as you go
stockinette stitch, seed stitch, increase, change color	Keiran, page 88	knit in the round
increase, knit in the round	Greta, page 36	make one increase purlwise
knit-on cast on, stockinette stitch, garter stitch	Lola, page 78	use a cable needle, single crochet
use a cable needle, stockinette stitch, increase and decrease	Ginger, page 60	
stockinette stitch, yarn over, increase and decrease	Frida, page 82	purl increase, double-centered decrease
stockinette stitch, knit in the round, rib, use a cable needle	Eleanor, page 32	
change color, stockinette stitch, increase and decrease	Eudora, page 106	
increase and decrease, yarn over	Ruby, page 100	read charts, block finished work

standard yarn weight system

Because there are so many different types of yarn and knitters, many folks found out that certain terms used to describe yarn weights weren't being universally applied. The Craft Yarn Council of America (CYCA) has introduced a Standard Yarn Weight System, hopefully to become a universal language when describing yarn.

You'll find the appropriate number in each pattern in order to best choose yarn if you need to use a substitute.

Yarn Weight Symbol & Category Names	1 SUPER FINE	2 FINE	3 LIGHT	4 MEDIUM	5 BULKY	6 SUPER BULKY
Type of Yarns in Category	Sock, Fingering, Baby	Sport, Baby	DK, Light Worsted	Worsted, Afghan, Aran	Chunky, Craft, Rug	Bulky, Roving
Knit Gauge Range* in Stockinette Stitch to 4 inches	27 to 32 sts	23 to 26 sts	21 to 24 sts	16 to 20 sts	12 to 15 sts	6 to 11 sts
Recommended Needle in Metric Size Range	2.25 to 3.25 mm	3.25 to 3.75 mm	3.75 to 4.5 mm	4.5 to 5.5 mm	5.5 to 8 mm	8mm and larger
Recommended Needle U.S. Size Range	1 to 3	3 to 5	5 to 7	7 to 9	9 to 11	11 and larger

* GUIDELINES ONLY: The above reflect the most commonly used gauges and needle or hook sizes for specific yarn categories

CIRCULAR VS. STRAIGHT

We admit it: we're fans of circular needles. The fact that circular needles can be used both for straight knitting (by knitting back and forth on the needle) and for circular knitting makes them not only flexible, but affordable as well—it's like getting two pairs of needles for the price of one. Circular needles can also accommodate more stitches than many straight needles, making them more useful in straight knitting when a large number of stitches are being knitted.

Many of our patterns are knit straight, meaning back and forth to create a flat piece. Others are knit circularly, forming a tube. On patterns where you must use circular needles, we've indictated that in the materials list. For the rest, we've just written the word "needles"; you can decide which you prefer to use.

Not sure how to use a circular needle for flat knitting?

To get an idea, try taking a pair of straight needles and tying a 10" length of yarn to the head of each needle. Now knit a small square with the needle ends tied together. You'll find that you knit exactly the same way, it's just that the needles are "attached." It's the same when using circular needles —when you're finished with a row all the stitches have moved from the left hand needle to the right hand needle. Now you simply switch hands—the needle with all the stitches goes back in your left hand and the empty needle begins in your right hand. And it's okay for the stitches to go onto the cord of the circular needle — they'll still stay the same size.

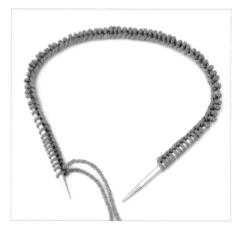

terms and abbreviations

begin, begins or beginning - **beg**

bind off - **BO**

8 stitch right slanting cable - **C8B**

contrasting color - **CC**

chain - **ch**

centimeters - **cm**

cable needle - **cn**

cast on - **CO**

continue - **cont**

decrease - **dec**

double pointed needle - **dpn**

grams - **g**

increase - **inc**

increase 1 or knit increase - **inc 1**

knit - **K**

knit into the front and back
of the stitch; knit increase - **k1-f/b**

knit 2 together - **k2tog**

knitwise - **kwise**

meters - **m**

make one, or lifted increase - **M1**

main color - **MC**

purl - **P**

purl into the front and back
of the stitch; purl increase - **p1-f/b**

purl next two stitches together - **p2tog**

pattern - **patt**

place marker - **pm**

pass the slipped stitch over - **psso**

purlwise - **pwise**

remain; remaining - **rem**

repeat - **rep**

Reverse Stockinette stitch - **Rev St st**

ribbing - **rib**

right side - **RS**

slip next two stitches, knit one,
pass the two slipped stitches over - **s2kp**

slip one stitch, knit the next stitch,
pass the slipped stitch over - **skp**

slip - **sl**

slip, slip knit,
or left leaning decrease - **ssk**

stitch marker - **sm**

Stockinette stitch - **St st**

wrong side - **WS**

put yarn to back of work - **yb**

bring yarn to front of work - **yf**

yarn over - **yo**

Continue in pattern, or just
keep on working as you have
been working until further
directions indicate to stop - **work even**

The 4- to 5-inch strand of yarn at either
the beginning or end of your knitting - **tail**

one-piece ponchos

SERAPES, RAGLANS, AND WRAP-AROUNDS

sanchez

ONE-PIECE SERAPE

SKILLS NEEDED
Knit and Purl
Pick Up Stitches

SKILLS LEARNED
Seed Stitch
Single Cast-On Method

sanchez

SQUARE SEED-STITCH SERAPE

Finished Measurements

36" wide x 22" long from neck to lower edge [folded in half]

Yarn

13 skeins Blue Sky Alpaca Bulky (50% alpaca, 50% wool; 45 yards/41 meters, 50 grams): super bulky alpaca or alpaca blend. Shown in color #1007 Gray Wolf.

Needles & Notions

US 17 (12.75 mm) 24" (60 cm) circular needle
US 17 (12.75 mm) 16" (40 cm) circular needle or size needed to obtain gauge
Yarn needle

Gauge

6 sts = 4" (10 cm) in Seed stitch

Pattern Stitch

Seed stitch (multiple of 2 stitches; 2 round repeat)
Row 1: * K1, P1; repeat from * to end of row.
Row 2: * P1, K1; repeat from * to end of row.
Repeat Rows 1 and 2 for entire length of poncho.

Serape

Using the longer circular needle, CO 66 stitches; working back and forth, begin Seed stitch. Continue working in Seed stitch until piece measures 22" from the beginning, ending with a WS row (32 rows have been worked).

ROW 33: Shape Neck: (RS) Work 23 stitches in Seed stitch; BO 20 stitches for neck opening, then continue to work in Seed stitch to the end (46 stitches remain; 23 stitches on each side of the neck opening).
ROW 34: Work 23 stitches in Seed stitch; CO 20 stitches for neck opening, using single cast-on method (see *Tricks & Techniques*, opposite); then continue to work in Seed stitch to the end (66 stitches). Continue to work in Seed stitch until piece measures 44" from the beginning (66 rows have been worked).
BO all stitches in Seed stitch.

Finishing

Lightly block, if necessary, to correct uneven tension. Heavy blocking will flatten texture.

Neck Band

With RS facing you and using the shorter circular needle, pick up and knit 40 stitches around the neck opening (see *Tricks & Techniques*, page 41). Place marker for beginning of round; begin Seed stitch. Work in Seed stitch for 2 rounds.
BO all stitches loosely in Seed stitch. Weave in ends.

tricks & techniques

Wrap the working yarn around your thumb from front to back.

Insert the needle up through the strand on your thumb.

Remove your thumb and forefinger. Yarn is looped around needle, forming a new stitch.

carson

ONE-PIECE SERAPE

SKILLS NEEDED
Stockinette Stitch
Increase
Decrease

SKILLS LEARNED
Pick Up Stitches

carson

ONE-PIECE SERAPE

Finished Measurements
40 ½" (103cm) x 47" (119 cm)

Yarn
10 balls Lana Grossa Elastico (96% cotton, 4% polyester; 173 yards/160 meters, 50 grams): fine weight yarn, cotton or cotton blend. Shown in color #34 Maize.

Needles & Notions
US 5 (3.75 mm) needles
US 5 (3.75 mm) 16" (40 cm) circular needle or size needed to obtain gauge
Yarn needle

Gauge
25 sts = 4" (10 cm) in Stockinette stitch (St st)

Body
CO 115 stitches for bottom edge; purl one row, work St st.

Shape Sides: (RS) * K1, inc 1, knit to last 2 sts, inc 1, k1. Purl 1 row. Continue in St st, repeat from * 54 times, increasing every other row (225 stitches); place a marker at each side to indicate end of shaping.

Measure poncho from bottom edge to marker. This is Measurement "A." Continue to work in St st until piece measures 24" from lower edge, ending with a WS row.

Shape Neck: (RS) Knit 76 stitches; BO 73 stitches for neck; knit remaining 76 stitches. Next Row: P76, cast on 73 stitches, p76 (225 stitches).

Continue in St st until piece measures the same as first half from neck to marker (24" minus Measurement "A"), ending with a WS row.

Shape Sides: (RS) * K1, ssk, knit to last 3 sts, k2tog, k1. Purl 1 row. Repeat from * 54 times, decreasing every other row (115 stitches). BO all stitches loosely.
Weave in ends.

Collar
Turn poncho inside out.
With RS of collar facing you [WS of poncho], and beginning at the right neck edge, use a 16" circular needle to pick up and knit 146 stitches around the neck (see *Tricks & Techniques*, opposite); do not join. Purl 1 row.

Continue in St st until collar measures 9" from pick-up row.
BO all stitches loosely.
Weave in ends.

Finishing
Turn poncho right-side out.
Block piece to finished measurements.
Fold down collar.

PICK UP STITCHES

With the right side of the work facing you, insert your needle into the center of the first stitch below your bind-off edge.

Wrap the yarn around your needle tip and draw it back through to the front.

You've picked up one stitch. Continue picking up stitches along the edge, being sure to space them out evenly to avoid any puckering.

eleanor

ONE-PIECE RAGLAN PONCHO

SKILLS NEEDED
Stockinette Stitch
Ribbing
Knit in the Round
Make One
Use a Cable Needle

eleanor

ONE-PIECE RAGLAN PONCHO

Finished Measurements

See schematic

Yarn

7 balls Rowan Polar (60% pure new wool 30% alpaca, 10% acrylic; 109 yards/100 meters, 100 grams): bulky weight alpaca and wool blend.
Shown in #645 Winter White.

Needles & Notions

US size 11 (8 mm) 16" (40 cm) circular needle
US size 11 (8 mm) 24" (60 cm) circular needle
or size needed to obtain gauge.
Change to the longer circular needle when stitches no longer fit comfortably on the shorter one.
4 stitch markers (sm), row counter, large cable needle (cn), yarn needle

Gauge

12 stitches = 4" (10 cm) in Stockinette stitch (St st)

Abbreviations

C8B (8-st right-slanting cable): Slip 4 stitches to cn, hold to back, k4, k4 from cn (see *Tricks & Techniques*, page 81).

Pattern Stitches

3x2 Rib (multiple of 5 sts; 1 round repeat)
Round 1: * K3, p2; repeat from * to end of round.
Repeat Round 1 for 3x2 Rib.

Cable (Panel 12 sts; 10-round repeat)
Round 1: P2, C8B, p2.
Rounds 2 to 10: P2, k8, p2.
Repeat Rounds 1 to 10 for Cable Panel.

Collar

Using shorter circular needle, CO 60 stitches; place a marker (pm) for beginning of round; join, being careful not to twist the stitches. Begin 3x2 rib.
Continue in pattern until piece measures 8" to 10" from the beginning, or desired length for collar.

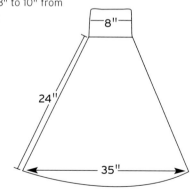

Body

Change to St st and Cable panel.

Establish Pattern: Beginning at marker, work Cable panel across next 12 stitches, pm; work 18 stitches in St st [knit every round]; pm, work cable panel across next 12 stitches, pm; work to end in St st.

Shape Body: (Round 2 of Cable panel) Continuing as established, on even-numbered rounds of Cable panel, M1 (increase) before first marker and after second marker at each side of the two Cable panels: 4 stitches will be increased on each even-numbered round.

Continue working odd-numbered rows as established, making a cable every tenth round, changing to the longer circular needle when stitches become too crowded on the shorter one. Continue as established until 100 rounds have been worked from the beginning of Body (10 sections of 10 rounds: 260 sts).

Bottom Edge

Change to 3x2 rib; beginning with p2, and work in rib for 4 rounds.

BO all stitches loosely in rib.

Finishing

Block piece to finished measurements, being careful not to flatten the cable or rib. Weave in the ends.

greta

ONE-PIECE PONCHO

SKILLS NEEDED
Knit in the Round
Increase Stitches
Change Colors (Optional)
Ribbing

SKILLS LEARNED
Make One Increase, Purlwise

greta

ONE-PIECE PONCHO

Finished Measurements

See schematic (page 40)

Yarn

GGH Soft Kid (70% super kid mohair, 25% nylon, 5% wool; 151 yards/140 meters, 50 grams) medium- to lightweight mohair.
Greta 1 (two-color version): 4 balls main color (MC); 4 balls contrast color (CC). Shown in color #69 Sunflower (yellow) (MC); #54 Green (CC).
Greta 2 (one-color version): 7 balls main color (MC). Shown in color #56 Plum Leaves (burgundy).

Needles & Notions

US size 6 (4 mm) 16" (40 cm) circular needle
US size 6 (4 mm) 24" (60 cm) circular needle
or size needed to obtain gauge. Change to longer needle when stitches no longer fit comfortably on shorter one.
Yarn needle

Gauge

20 stitches = 4" (10 cm) in Stockinette stitch (St st)

Abbreviations

M1: Make one increase, knitwise
M1-p: Make one increase, purlwise (see Tricks & Techniques, page 41)

Body

Using the shorter circular needle and MC, CO 100 sts for neck edge, pm for beginning of round; join, being careful not to twist stitches.
ROUNDS 1 to 9: Knit [St st].
ROUND 10: For Greta 1 * With MC, k10 [St st], with CC, M1-p [Rev St st]; repeat from * to beginning of round.
For Greta 2 * K10 [St st], M1-p [Rev St st]; repeat from * to beginning of round (110 sts).
ROUNDS 11 to 14: Continue in color(s) as established for remainder of piece: * k10, p1; repeat from * to beginning of round.
ROUND 15: * K10, M1 [St st], p1; repeat from * to beginning of round (120 sts).
ROUNDS 16 to 19: * K11, p1; repeat from * to beginning of round.
ROUND 20: * K11, M1-p, p1; repeat from * to beginning of round (130 sts).
ROUNDS 21 to 29: * K11, p2; repeat from * to beginning of round.
ROUND 30: * K11, M1-p, p2; repeat from * to beginning of round (140 sts).
ROUNDS 31 to 34: * K11, p3; repeat from * to beginning of round.
ROUND 35: * K11, M1, p3; repeat from * to beginning of round (150 sts).
ROUNDS 36 to 39: * K12, p3; repeat from * to beginning of round.
ROUND 40: * K12, M1-p, p3; repeat from * to beginning of round (160 sts).
ROUNDS 41 to 49: * K12, p4; repeat from * to beginning of round.
ROUND 50: * K12, M1-p, p4; repeat from * to beginning of round (170 sts).
ROUNDS 51 to 54: * K12, p5; repeat from * to beginning of round.
ROUND 55: * K12, M1, p5; repeat from * to beginning of round (180 sts).
ROUNDS 56 to 59: * K13, p5; repeat from * to beginning of round.
ROUND 60: * K13, M1-p, p5; repeat from * to beginning of round (190 sts).
ROUNDS 61 to 69: * K13, p6; repeat from * to beginning of round.

ROUND 70: * K13, M1-p, p6; repeat from * to beginning of round (200 sts).
ROUNDS 71 to 74: * K13, p7; repeat from * to beginning of round.
ROUND 75: * K13, M1, p7; repeat from * to beginning of round (210 sts).
ROUNDS 76 to 79: * K14, p7; repeat from * to beginning of round.
ROUND 80: * K14, M1-p, p7; repeat from * to beginning of round (220 sts).
ROUNDS 81 to 89: * K14, p8; repeat from * to beginning of round.
ROUND 90: * K14, M1-p, p8; repeat from * to beginning of round (230 sts).
ROUNDS 91 to 94: * K14, p9; repeat from * to beginning of round.
ROUND 95: * K14, M1, p9; repeat from * to beginning of round (240 sts).
ROUNDS 96 to 99: * K15, p9; repeat from * to beginning of round.
ROUND 100: * K15, M1-p, K9; repeat from * to beginning of round (250 sts).
ROUNDS 101 to 109: * K15, p10; repeat from * to beginning of round.
ROUND 110: * K15, M1-p, p10; repeat from * to beginning of round (260 sts).
ROUNDS 111 to 114: * K15, p11; repeat from * to beginning of round.
ROUND 115: * K15, M1, p11; repeat from * to beginning of round (270 sts).
ROUNDS 116 to 119: * K16, p11; repeat from * to beginning of round.
ROUND 120: * K16, M1-p, p11; repeat from * to beginning of round (280 sts).
ROUNDS 121 to 129: * K16, p12; repeat from * to beginning of round.
ROUND 130: * K16, M1-p, p12; repeat from * to beginning of round (290 sts).
For Greta 1, BO all stitches loosely; for Greta 2, continue in pattern.

ROUNDS 131 to 134: * K16, p13; repeat from * to beginning of round.
ROUND 135: * K16, M1, p13; repeat from * to beginning of round (300 sts).
ROUNDS 136 to 139: * K17, p13; repeat from * to beginning of round.
ROUND 140: * K17, M1-p, p13; repeat from * to beginning of round (310 sts).
ROUNDS 141 to 149: * K17, p14; repeat from * to beginning of round.
ROUND 150: * K17, M1-p, p14; repeat from * to beginning of round (320 sts).
ROUNDS 151 to 154: * K17, p15; repeat from * to beginning of round.
ROUND 155: * K17, M1, p15; repeat from * to beginning of round (330 sts).
ROUNDS 156 to 159: * K18, p15; repeat from * to beginning of round.
ROUND 160: K18, M1-p, p15; repeat from * to beginning of round (340 sts).
ROUNDS 161 to 169: * K18, p16; repeat from * to beginning of round.
For Greta 2, BO all stitches loosely.

Finishing

Block piece to finished measurements.

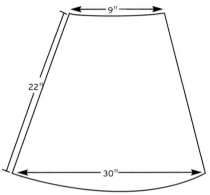

Greta 1 Cowl Neck: Turn poncho inside out. With WS of garment facing you [RS of cowl], using the shorter needle and MC, pick up and knit 100 stitches around Neck Edge (see page 30); work Rows 1 to 40 as for Body, using MC only throughout the entire cowl neck. BO all stitches loosely in pattern. Weave in ends.

Greta 2 Hood: With RS facing you, using the shorter circular needle and MC, begin on Stitch 7 of the bound-off stitches of the Front Neck Edge (7th stitch after beginning of round on Body) and pick up and knit 43 stitches (see page 30); place a marker for Center Back; then pick up and knit another 43 stitches, ending 7 stitches before beginning of round on Body. There are 14 stitches at Center Front left unworked; 86 live stitches. Turn; purl 1 (WS) row. You will be working back and forth on circular needle using MC throughout.

Establish Pattern: (RS) Work first 5 stitches in 1x1 Rib (see page 116), beginning and ending k1; work in St st to last 5 stitches; work last 5 stitches in 1x1 rib, beginning and ending k1. Work even for 3", ending with a WS row.
Shape Hood: Increase 1 stitch at each side of marker every 7 rows 8 times, then every 8 rows 3 times (108 stitches).
Continue working in pattern until Hood measures 13" from pick up row. BO all stitches loosely in pattern, then sew seam at top of hood. Weave in ends.

tricks & techniques

MAKE ONE INCREASE, PURLWISE (M1-P)

Insert left needle from front to back through the horizontal strand between the two stitches.

This strand is now on your left needle. Insert right needle tip into it from back to front.

Go ahead and purl it. It will seem awkward, but purling it through the back loop twists the stitch, keeping a hole from forming.

mash

ONE-PIECE WRAP-AROUND PONCHO

SKILLS NEEDED
Yarn Over
Decrease

SKILLS LEARNED
Alternative Cast On: Knit-On

mash

ONE PIECE WRAP-AROUND PONCHO

Finished Measurements
One Panel: 24" wide x 70" long

Yarn
3 balls Colinette Giotto (50% cotton, 40% rayon, 10% nylon; 156 yards/144 meters, 100 grams): super bulky ribbon. Shown in #077 Dusk (camouflage).

Needles & Notions
US 15 (10 mm) needles or size needed to obtain gauge
Yarn needle

Gauge
5 sts = 4" (10 cm) in Picot stitch

Pattern Stitch
Picot stitch (multiple of 2 stitches; 4 row repeat)
Row 1 (RS): K1, * yo, k2tog; repeat from * to last stitch, k1.
Row 2: Purl.
Row 3: K2, * yo, k2tog; repeat from * to end of row.
Row 4: Purl.
Repeat Rows 1 to 4 for Picot stitch.

Poncho
CO 30 stitches; begin Picot stitch.
Continue working in pattern until piece measures 70" from the beginning, or to desired length; ending with a WS row.
BO all stitches loosely.
Weave in ends.

Finishing
Do not block (blocking will flatten texture).
Sew "A" to "B" matching points "o" to "o" and "x" to "x."

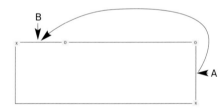

ALTERNATIVE CAST ON TECHNIQUE:
KNIT-ON

Make a slip knot on left-hand needle.
* Insert right-hand needle into stitch on left-hand needle and knit one stitch, but do not drop stitch from left-hand needle; slip new stitch knitwise from right-hand needle to left-hand needle. Repeat from * for number of stitches to be cast on.

This makes a flexible, neat edge.

desirée

ONE-PIECE WRAP-AROUND PONCHO

SKILLS NEEDED
Yarn Over
Right Slanting Decrease

SKILLS LEARNED
Add Fringe

desirée

ONE-PIECE WRAP-AROUND PONCHO

Finished Measurements
One panel: 17" wide x 53" long

Yarn
4 balls Cascade Pima Tencel (50% tencel, 50% pima cotton; 110 yards/101 meters, 50 grams): lightweight cotton blend. Shown in color #1317 Rose.

Needles & Notions
US 9 (5.5 mm) needles or size needed to obtain gauge
Yarn needle, crochet hook size I/9 (5.5 mm) for fringe

Gauge
16 stitches = 4" (10 cm) in Brioche stitch

Pattern Stitch
Brioche stitch (multiple of 3 sts; 1 row repeat)
Row 1 (Preparation Row): * Yo, sl 1, k1; repeat from * to end of row.
Row 2: * Yo, sl 1, k2tog; repeat from * to end of row.
Repeat Row 2 for Brioche stitch.

Poncho
CO 66 stitches; begin Brioche stitch.
Continue in pattern until piece measures 53", or desired length.
BO all stitches loosely.
Weave in ends.

Finishing
Block piece to finished measurements.
Sew "A" to "B" matching points "o" to "o" and "x" to "x."

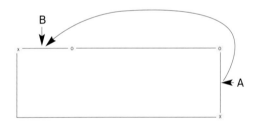

Add fringe: cut 228 pieces of yarn, each 11" long, to be used as fringe. Using 2 strands held together, fold strands in half and loop through the bottom edge of the poncho (see *Tricks & Techniques*, opposite), spacing fringe every other stitch. Continue around the entire bottom edge.

note:
For yo at beginning of row in Brioche stitch pattern, hold yarn to front of work as if to purl. Slip first stitch, then k2tog, being careful to hold yo in position in front of the slipped stitch, so it doesn't slip out of place.

tricks & techniques

ADD FRINGE

Cut strands of yarn to twice the desired length. Insert crochet hook through the bottom edge of the garment, loop strand(s) around the hook, and pull through edge. Insert tail ends through loop and pull tight, forming a slipknot.
So fancy!

gilda

ONE-PIECE PONCHO

SKILLS NEEDED
Garter Stitch
Yarn Over

SKILLS LEARNED
Drop Stitches on Purpose

gilda

ONE-PIECE PONCHO

Finished Measurements
One Panel: 18" wide x 60" long

Yarn
4 balls Crystal Palace Glam (36% acrylic, 35% rayon, 15% wool, 14% nylon; 87 yards/80 meters; 50 grams): bulky (#5) rayon-blend tape. Shown in color #9354 Henna Glow.

Needles and Notions
US size 17 (12.75mm) needle or size needed to obtain gauge
Yarn needle

Gauge
8 stitches = 4" (10 cm) in Garter stitch

Poncho
CO 36 stitches
ROWS 1 through 6: Knit all stitches.
ROW 7: * K1, yo; repeat from * to end of row.
ROW 8: Knit across, dropping yarn overs.
Repeat Rows 1 through 8 until piece measures 60" from the beginning, ending with Row 6.
BO all stitches loosely. Weave in ends.

Finishing
Do not block (blocking will flatten the texture).
Fold in half lengthwise matching "x" to "x" and "o" to "o."
Sew up seam in between "x"s and "o"s, leaving space for your head.

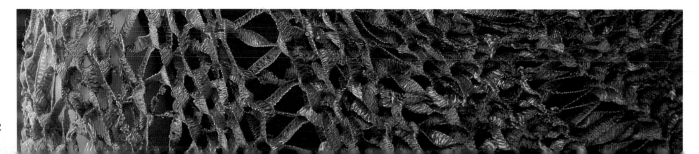

tricks & techniques

DROP STITCHES ON PURPOSE

Just when you think you've gotten a handle on your knitting and you're no longer dropping stitches, you'll come across a pattern that tells you to drop them on purpose.

Some stitch patterns use a stitch a few rows down that halts the one dropped at a specific place. Other patterns use long running strands of dropped stitches as design elements.

Another common use of stitch "dropping" involves yarn overs, where the additional strands of the yarn over(s) are "dropped" off the needle purposefully in the following row, creating long strands of yarn surrounded by stitches, as in this pattern.

two-piece ponchos

SEMICIRCLES AND RECTANGLES

tessa

TWO-PIECE PONCHO

SKILLS NEEDED
Knit

SKILLS LEARNED
Garter Stitch
Right-Slanting Decrease
Left-Slanting Decrease
Knit Increase

tessa

TWO-PIECE PONCHO

Finished Measurements
See schematic

Yarn
7 skeins Colinette Point 5 (100% pure wool; 54 yards/50 meters, 100 grams): super bulky. Shown in color #137 Banwy (variegated blues, purples, and grays).

Needles & Notions
US 19 (15 mm) needles or size needed to obtain gauge
Yarn needle

Gauge
7.5 sts = 4" (10 cm) in Garter stitch

Abbreviation
k1-f/b: Increase 1 stitch by knitting through the front and the back (see *Tricks & Techniques*, opposite).
ssk: Slip, slip, knit (see tricks & techniques, opposite).
k2tog: Knit two stitches together (see *Tricks & Techniques*, opposite).

Pattern Stitch
Garter stitch (any number of stitches; 1 row repeat)
All rows: Knit every stitch.

Panels (make two)
CO 4 stitches; begin Garter stitch.

Increase Section: Bottom
ROW 1: K1, k1-f/b, k2, k1-f/b, k1 (6 stitches).
ROW 2: K1, k1-f/b, k4, k1-f/b, k1 (8 stitches).
Continue in Garter stitch as established, increasing after first stitch and before last stitch, until 70 stitches have been increased (74 stitches).

Decrease Section, Part One: Middle
ROW 1: Knit.
ROW 2: K1, ssk, knit to last 3 stitches, k2tog, k1.
Repeat Rows 1 and 2 eight times (56 stitches remain).

Decrease Section, Part Two: Top
ROW 1: K1, ssk, knit to last 3 stitches, k2tog, k1.
Repeat Row 1 until 20 stitches remain.
Bind off all stitches loosely.
Weave in ends.

Finishing
Lightly block pieces to finished measurements. Sew the two panels together at their top edges along each side of the bound-off neck edge.

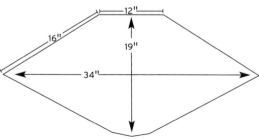

tricks & techniques

INCREASE

Knit Increase: (k1-f/b) knit through the front and back of the stitch.
Insert needle knitwise into next stitch on left-hand needle; wrap the
yarn around the needle and bring right-hand needle tip to the front as
you normally would, but do not remove the stitch from the left-hand
needle. Now insert the tip of your right-hand needle into the back of
the same stitch on the left-hand needle and knit; remove both stitches
to the right-hand needle.

DECREASE

Left-slanting decrease: Slip, slip, knit (ssk).
Slip the next two stitches, one at a time,
from the left to the right needle. Insert
left needle tip into the front of these two
stitches (see photo below) and knit them
together.

Right-slanting decrease: knit two together
(k2tog). Insert right needle into the next two
stitches on the left needle (see photo below)
and knit them together.

ginger

TWO-PIECE PONCHO

SKILLS NEEDED
Use a Cable Needle
Stockinette Stitch
Garter Stitch
Increase
Decrease

ginger

TWO-PIECE PONCHO

Finished Measurements

See schematic (page 64)

Yarn   or

5 skeins Cascade Pastaza (50% llama, 50% wool; 132 yards/121 meters, 100 grams): medium-weight llama or alpaca blend; shown in color #1107 Pale Sky (A)
OR
3 skeins Brown Sheep Cotton Fleece (80% cotton/20% merino wool; 215 yards/197 meters, 100 grams): lightweight cotton or cotton-blend yarn; shown in color #CW-100 Cotton Ball (B).

Needles & Notions

US size 9 (5.5 mm) needle (A)
US size 9 (5.5 mm) 16" (40 cm) circular needle for neck (A)
US size 6 (4 mm) needle (B)
US size 6 (4 mm) 16" (40 cm) circular needle for neck (B)
or size needed to obtain gauge
Row counter, medium cable needle (cn) for Pastaza, small for cotton fleece, two stitch markers, stitch holder, straight pins

Gauge

16 stitches = 4" (10 cm) in Reverse Stockinette stitch (Rev St st), using larger needles and A
20 stitches = 4" (10 cm) in Reverse Stockinette stitch (Rev St st), using smaller needles and B

Abbreviations

FC (Front Cross): Slip next stitch to cn and hold in front, p1, then k1 from cn.
BC (Back Cross): Slip next stitch to cn and hold in back, k1, then p1 from cn.

Pattern Stitch

Reverse Stockinette stitch (Rev St st): Purl all stitches on RS, knit all stitches on WS.

Back of Poncho

CO 136 stitches; begin Garter stitch.
Work in Garter stitch for 6 rows, ending with a WS row.
Change to Rev St st; work for 3 rows, ending with a RS row (9 rows total).

Shape Body: Continuing in St st, decrease 1 stitch each side this row, then every 4 rows 26 times as follows:
ROW 10 (WS): K1, k2tog, knit across to last 3 sts, slip 1, k1, psso (skp), k1. Continuing in St st, work for 3 rows. Continue as established until 115 rows have been worked, ending with a WS row (82 stitches remain).
ROW 116 (WS): [K1, k2tog] twice, knit across to last 6 stitches, [skp, k1] twice (78 stitches remain).
Work for 3 rows, ending with a WS row.

ROW 120 (WS): [K1, k2 tog] three times, knit across to last 9 stitches, [skp, k1] three times (72 stitches remain).

ROW 121: Purl.

ROW 122: [K1, k2tog] four times, knit across to last 12 stitches, [skp, k1] (64 stitches remain)

ROW 123: P32 (to center), pm, purl to end.

Shape Shoulder and Neck

ROW 124 (WS): BO 8 sts at shoulder edge, knit across to marker, place the remaining sts on a holder; turn.

ROW 125: BO 5 sts at neck edge, purl to end.

ROW 126: BO 8 sts, knit to end.

ROW 127: BO 3 sts, purl to end.

ROW 128: BO remaining stitches.
Return stitches from holder to needle, ready to work a WS row.

ROW 124: Knit to end.

ROW 125: BO 8 sts, purl to end.

ROW 126: BO 5 sts, knit to end.

ROW 127: BO 8 sts, purl to end.

ROW 128: BO 3 sts, knit to end.
BO remaining stitches in 1x1 rib.
Weave in ends.

Front of Poncho

CO 136 stitches; begin Garter stitch.
Work in Garter stitch for 6 rows, ending with a WS row.
Change to Rev St st; work for 3 rows, ending with a RS row (9 rows total).

Shape Body: Continuing in Rev St st, decrease 1 stitch each side this row, then every 4 rows 26 times as follows:

ROW 10 (WS): K1, k2tog, knit across to last 3 sts, slip 1, k1, psso (skp), k1. Continuing in Rev St st, work for 3 rows.
Continue shaping as established until 115 rows have been worked, ending with a WS row (82 stitches remain).

AND AT THE SAME TIME
When piece measures 12" from the beginning, ending with Row 66, begin Anchor section as follows:

ROW 67: P37, pm, p15, k2, p15, pm, purl to end.

Below are the instructions for the section between the stitch markers; continue shaping as established, working Rev St st each side of markers.

ROW 68: K15, p2, k15.

ROW 69: P14, slip next st to cable needle and hold in back, k1, k1 from cn; slip next st to cn and hold in front, k1, k1 from cn; p14.

ROW 70: K13, FC, p2, BC, k13.

ROW 71: P12, BC, p1, k2, p1, FC, p12.

ROW 72: K11, FC, k2, p2, k2, BC, k11.

ROW 73: P10, BC, p3, k2, p3, FC, p10.

ROW 74: K9, FC, k4, p2, k4, BC, k9.

ROW 75: P8, BC, p5, k2, p5, FC, p8.

ROW 76: K7, FC, k6, p2, k6, BC, k7.

ROW 77: P6, BC, p7, k2, p7, FC, p6.

ROW 78: K5, FC, k8, p2, k8, BC, k5.

ROW 79: P4, BC, p9, k2, p9, FC, p4.

ROW 80: K1, p7, k7, p2, k7, p7, k1.

ROW 81: P1, FC, k3, BC, p7, k2, p7, FC, k3, BC, p1.

ROW 82: K2, p5, k8, p2, k8, p5, k2.

ROW 83: P2, FC, k1, BC, p8, k2, p8, FC, k1, BC, p2.

ROW 84: K3, p3, k9, p2, k9, p3, k3.

ROW 85: P3, m1-p, slip 1, k2tog, psso, m1-p; p9, k2, p9, m1-p; slip 1, k2tog, psso, m1-p; p3.

ROW 86: K4, p1, k10, p2, k10, p1, k4.

ROW 87: P10, k12, p10.

ROW 88: K10, p12, k10.

ROW 89: Repeat Row 87.

ROW 90: Repeat Row 88.

ROW 91: P15, k2, p15.

ROW 92: K15, p2, k15.

ROW 93: Repeat Row 91.

ROW 94: Repeat Row 92.

ROW 95: P15, slip next stitch to cn and hold in front, k1, then k1 from cn; p15.

ROW 96: K14, FC, BC, k14.

ROW 97: P13, BC, p2, FC, p13.

ROW 98: K12, FC, k4, BC, k12.

ROW 99: P12, k1, p6, k1, p12.

ROW 100: K12, p1, k6, p1, k12.

ROW 101: P12, FC, p4, BC, p12.

ROW 102: K13, BC, k2, FC, k13.

ROW 103: P14, FC, BC, p14.

ROW 104: K15; skip 1 stitch and purl the 2nd stitch then purl the skipped stitch and slip both stitches from the needle together; k15.

ROW 105: Purl, removing stitch markers.

ROW 106: Knit.

ROWS 107-115: Continue in Rev St st, completing shaping.

ROWS 116-128: Work as for Back.

Collar

Pin the sides of the front and back pieces together, with the right side out; leave room at the neck to pick up stitches. With RS facing you and beginning at the side of the neck opening, use a 16" circular needle to pick up and knit 80 sts around the neck. Join, placing a marker at shoulder seam.

ROUND 1: Purl, placing another marker after 40 stitches (at other shoulder seam).

ROUND 2: K1, k2tog, knit to marker, k2tog, knit to end.

ROUND 3: P1, p2tog, purl to marker, p2tog, purl to end.

ROUND 4: K1, k2tog, knit to marker, k2tog, knit to end.

ROUND 5: P1, p2tog, purl to marker, p2tog, purl to end.

ROUND 6: K1, k2tog, knit to marker, k2tog, knit to end.

Bind off all stitches.

Weave in ends.

Finishing

Block to finished measurements.

Sew up side seams starting from the top of the collar down to the edge.

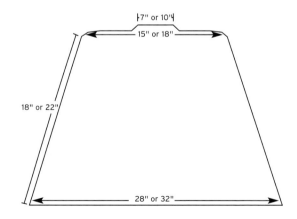

sonya

TWO-PIECE RECTANGULAR PONCHO

SKILLS NEEDED
Knit and Purl
Cast On
Bind Off

SKILLS LEARNED
Stockinette Stitch
Cast On or Bind Off Loosely

sonya

TWO-PIECE RECTANGULAR PONCHO

Finished Measurements

Two panels: each with a length equaling 29" (34").

Width will vary due to flexible gauge.

Yarn

3 balls Lana Grossa Meilenweit Cotton Fun & Stripes (45% cotton, 42% new wool, 13% polyamide; 205 yards/190 meters, 50 grams): super fine wool blend; shown in color #345 Orange Kool Aid

OR

3 balls Lana Grossa Meilenweit Fun (80% virgin wool, 20% nylon; 454 yards/420 meters, 50 grams): super fine wool blend; shown in color #83 Rainbow Royale.

Needles & Notions

US 13 (9 mm) needle for smaller poncho

US 15 (10 mm) needle for larger poncho

Yarn needle

Gauge

11 stitches = 4 inches (10 cm) in Stockinette stitch (St st), using larger needle

14 stitches = 4 inches (10 cm) in Stockinette stitch (St st), using smaller needle

Gauge is very flexible.

Pattern Stitch

Stockinette stitch (any number of sts; 2 row repeat)

Row 1: (RS) Knit all stitches.

Row 2: Purl all stitches.

Repeat Rows 1 and 2 for St st.

Panels (make two)

Loosely CO 80 stitches; begin St st.

Continue working in St st until piece measures 29" (34") from the beginning.

BO all stitches loosely.

Weave in ends.

Finishing

Lightly block, if necessary, to correct uneven tension.

Sew the two panels together (see the Mae schematic on page 72).

tricks & techniques

CAST ON (CO) OR BIND OFF (BO) LOOSELY

Often a pattern will ask that you cast on loosely or bind off loosely. A great way to do this is to use a larger needle size when casting on or binding off. This creates a consistent, loose edge without having to rely on your tension.

mae

TWO-PIECE RECTANGULAR PONCHO

SKILLS NEEDED
Stockinette Stitch
Knit-On Cast On

SKILLS LEARNED
Change Colors
Weave in the Ends As You Go

mae

TWO-PIECE RECTANGULAR PONCHO

Finished Measurements

Two Panels, each measuring 21" wide x 37" long

Yarn

Crystal Palace Merino Frappe (80% merino, 20% polyamide; 140 yards/129 meters, 50 grams): medium-weight mohair blend.
One ball each of six colors, shown in:
A) Mexican Chocolate (color 046)
B) Olive (color 089)
C) Sage (color 020B)
D) Deep Plum (color 40B)
E) Cranberry (color 031B)
F) Mink (color 024)

Needles & Notions

US 11 (8 mm) needles or size needed to obtain gauge
Yarn needle

Gauge

12 sts = 4" (10 cm) in Stockinette stitch (St st)

Stripe Sequence (shown)

In St st, * work 6 rows of each color as follows, weaving in the ends as you go (see *Tricks & Techniques*, opposite):
A, B, C, D, E and F; repeat from * to suggested length.

Panels (make two)

Using Knit-On Cast On (see *Tricks & Techniques*, page 45), CO 120 sts;
begin Stripe Sequence (either use sequence given or create your own).
Continue working in Stripe Sequence until a total of 108 rows have been worked;
3 repeats of Stripe Sequence are shown.
BO all stitches loosely.
Weave in ends.

Finishing

Block pieces to finished measurements.
Sew side A1 to side B1
and side A2 to side B2.

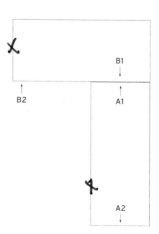

tricks & techniques

CHANGE COLOR

Insert right-hand needle into next stitch; instead of using original color, take the free end of the new color and lay it between the needles, leaving a 4" to 6" tail. Complete stitch, using new color. Continue knitting with your new color.

WEAVE IN THE ENDS AS YOU GO

Knit one stitch using new color; lay tail over working yarn. Knit next stitch.

By continuing to lay the tail over the working yarn before each stitch, the tail becomes woven into the back (WS) of the work.

Once you have woven in 2" to 3" of tail, trim the end.

amelia

TWO-PIECE RECTANGULAR PONCHO

SKILLS NEEDED
Ribbing

SKILLS LEARNED
Use a Repeating Pattern Stitch

amelia

TWO-PIECE RECTANGULAR PONCHO

Finished Measurements

Two panels, each measuring approximately 21½" x 31"

Yarn 5

10 balls GGH Aspen (50% merino wool, 50% microfiber; 62 yards/57 meters, 50 grams): bulky wool blend. Shown in color #17 Grape.

Needles

US 11 (8 mm) needles or size needed to obtain gauge
Yarn needle

Gauge

10 sts = 4" (10 cm) in Brocade stitch

Pattern Stitch

1x1 Rib (multiple of 2 stitches; 1 row repeat)
Row 1: *K1, p1; repeat from * to end of row.
Repeat Row 1 for 1x1 rib.

Panels (make 2)

CO 53 stitches; work 1x1 rib for first two rows (border).
Begin Pattern: Brocade stitch (multiple of 12 stitches + 5; 12 row repeat)
ROW 1 (RS): K1, p1, k1, * p1, k9, p1, k1; repeat from * to last 2 stitches, p1, k1.
ROW 2: K1, p1, k1, * p1, k1, p7, k1, p1, k1; repeat from * to last 2 stitches, p1, k1.
ROW 3: K1, p1, k1, * p1, k1, p1, k5, [p1, k1] twice; repeat from * to last 2 stitches, p1, k1.
ROW 4: K1, p2, * [p1, k1] twice, p3, k1, p1, k1, p2; repeat from * to last 2 stitches, p1, k1.
ROW 5: K1, p1, k1, * k2, [p1, k1] 3 times, p1, k3; repeat from * to last 2 stitches, p1, k1.
• **ROW 6:** K1, p2, * p3, [k1, p1] twice, k1, p4; repeat from * to last 2 stitches, p1, k1.
ROW 7: K1, p1, k1, * k4, p1, k1, p1, k5; repeat from * to last 2 stitches, p1, k1.
ROW 8: K1, p2, * p3, [k1, p1] twice, k1, p4; repeat from * to last 2 stitches, p1, k1.
ROW 9: K1, p1, k1, * k2, [p1, k1] 3 times, p1, k3; repeat from * to last 2 stitches, p1, k1.
ROW 10: K1, p2, * [p1, k1] twice, p3, k1, p1, k1, p2; repeat from * to last 2 stitches, p1, k1.
ROW 11: K1, p1, k1, * p1, k1, p1, k5, [p1, k1] twice; repeat from * to last 2 stitches, p1, k1.
ROW 12: K1, p1, k1, * p1, k1, p7, k1, p1, k1; repeat from * to last 2 stitches, p1, k1.
Repeat Rows 1 through 12 until piece measures approximately 31" from the beginning, ending with Row 6 or Row 12.
Change to 1x1 rib; work even for last two rows (border).
BO all stitches loosely in rib. Weave in ends.

Finishing

Block pieces to finished measurements. Sew panels together (see Mae schematic, page 72).

lola

TWO-PIECE RECTANGULAR PONCHO

SKILLS NEEDED
Knit-On Cast On
Stockinette Stitch
Garter Stitch

SKILLS LEARNED
Make a Cable
Single Crochet

lola

TWO-PIECE RECTANGULAR PONCHO

Finished Measurements

Two panels, each measuring 44" long x 18" wide

Yarn

5 balls of Rowan Cork (95% merino, 5% nylon; 120 yards/110 meters, 50 grams): bulky wool or wool blend.
Shown in color #045 Snuggle (tan).

Needles & Notions

US 36 (19 mm) or size needed to obtain gauge
Extra-large cable needle (cn), yarn needle, crochet hook size N/P-15 (10 mm)

Gauge

8 stitches = 4" (10 cm) in Pattern stitch.

Abbreviations

C8F (8-stitch left-slanting cable): Slip 4 sts to cn and hold in front, k4, knit 4 from cn.
C8B (8-stitch right-slanting cable): Slip 4 sts to cn and hold in back, k4, knit 4 from cn.

Pattern Stitch

(worked over 60 sts; 12 row repeat)
Row 1 and all WS rows: K12, p12, k12, p12, k12.
Rows 2, 4, 8, and 10: K2, p10, k12, p12, k12, p10, k2.
Row 6: K2, p10, C8F, k4, p12, C8F, k4, p10, k2.
Row 12: K2, p10, k4, C8B, p12, k4, C8B, p10, k2.
Repeat Rows 1 through 12 for Pattern stitch.

Panels (make two)

Using Knit-On Cast On (see *tricks & techniques*, page 45), CO 60 stitches.
Knit all stitches for the first two rows (border).
Change to Pattern stitch; work Rows 1 through 12 four times (48 rows).
Knit all stitches for the last two rows (border).
BO all stitches loosely.

Weave in ends.

Finishing

Lightly block to finished measurements, if necessary, to correct uneven tension.
Sew 2 panels together (see Mae schematic, page 72).
Neck Edging: Using crochet hook, work 1 row

note:

Single crochet will tighten the neck and make a neat edge. Beginning at one seam, insert crochet hook into first stitch along the neck edge, bring the yarn over the hook and pull it through. *Insert the hook into the next stitch and draw through a second loop. Bring the yarn over and pull through both loops on the hook. Repeat from * to end of row.

USE A CABLE NEEDLE

It's simpler than it looks. Just slip the number of stitches indicated in the instructions onto a separate needle (either a cable needle [cn] or a double-pointed needle [dpn]).

Hold the stitches on the cable needle, either to the front or back as indicated in the instructions. Knit the number of stitches indicated in the instructions from the left-hand needle to the right hand needle.

Then knit the slipped stitches from the cable needle.

frida

TWO-PIECE RECTANGULAR PONCHO

SKILLS NEEDED
Stockinette Stitch
Yarn Over
Increase
Decrease

SKILLS LEARNED
Purl Increase
Double-Centered Decrease

frida

TWO-PIECE RECTANGULAR PONCHO

Finished Measurements
Two panels: each measuring 19" wide x 30" long

Yarn
2 skeins Tess Designer Yarns Silk and Merino (50% silk, 50% merino; 250 yards/230 meters, 100 grams): medium-weight wool blend. Shown in Tangerine.

Needles & Notions
US 8 (5 mm) needles or size needed to obtain gauge
Yarn needle

Gauge
18 sts = 4" (10 cm) in Pattern stitch

Abbreviations
P1-f/b: (RS) Purl into the front and back of the stitch (see *tricks & techniques*, opposite)
S2Kp (double-centered decrease): (RS) Slip 2 stitches knitwise, k1, pass 2 slipped stitches over knit stitch (see *tricks & techniques*, opposite)
Yo: Yarn over

Panels (make two)
CO 90 stitches; work in Pattern stitch as follows:
ROW 1 (WS): K37, p5, k4, p3, k41.
ROW 2: K32, p7, p2tog, k1-f/b, k2, p4, k2, yo, k1, yo, k2, p5, k32 (92 stitches).
ROW 3: K37, p7, k4, p2, k1, p1, k40.
ROW 4: K32, p6, p2tog, k1, p1-f/b, k2, p4, k3, yo, k1, yo, k3, p5, k32 (94 stitches).
ROW 5: K37, p9, k4, p2, k2, p1, k39.
ROW 6: K32, p5, p2tog, k1, p1-f/b, p1, k2, p4, ssk, k5, k2tog, p5, k32 (92 stitches).
ROW 7: K37, p7, k4, p2, k3, p1, k38.
ROW 8: K32, p4, p2tog, k1, p1-f/b, p2, k2, p4, ssk, k3, k2tog, p5, k32 (90 stitches).
ROW 9: K37, p5, k4, p2, k4, p1, k37.
ROW 10: K32, p5, yo, k1, yo, p4, k2, p4 ssk, k1, k2tog, p5, k32.
ROW 11: K37, p3, k4, p2, k4, p3, k37.
ROW 12: K32, p5, [k1, yo] twice, k1, p4, k1, M1, k1, p2tog, p2, s2Kp, p5, k32.
ROW 13: K41, p3, k4, p5, k37.
ROW 14: K32, p5, k2, yo, k1, yo, k2, p4, k1, k1-f/b, k1, p2tog, p7, k32 (92 stitches).
ROW 15: K40, p1, k1, p2, k4, p7, k37.
ROW 16: K32, p5, k3, yo, k1, yo, k3, p4, k2, p1-f/b, k1, p2tog, p6, k32 (94 stitches).
ROW 17: K39, p1, k2, p2, k4, p9, k37.
ROW 18: K32, p5, ssk, k5, k2tog, p4, k2, p1, p1-f/b, k1, p2tog, p5, k32 (92 stitches).
ROW 19: K38, p1, k3, p2, k4, p7, k37.
ROW 20: K32, p5, ssk, k3, k2tog, p4, k2, p2, p1-f/b, k1, p2tog, p4, k32 (90 stitches).

ROW 21: K37, p1, k4, p2, k4, p5, k37.

ROW 22: K32, p5, ssk, k1, k2tog, p4, k2, p4, yo, k1, yo, p5, k32.

ROW 23: K37, p3, k4, p2, k4, p3, k37.

ROW 24: K32, p5, S2KP, p2, p2tog, k1, M1, k1, p4, [k1, yo] twice, k1, p5, k32.

Repeat Rows 1 through 24 until piece measures 30" from the beginning.

BO all stitches loosely.

Weave in ends.

Finishing

Block pieces to finished measurements.

Sew panels together (see Mae schematic, page 72).

tricks & techniques

PURL INCREASE: PURL THROUGH THE FRONT AND BACK OF THE STITCH (P1-F/B)

Insert the right-hand needle purlwise into the next stitch on the left-hand needle; wrap the yarn around the needle and bring right-hand needle tip to the back as you normally would to form a purl stitch, but do not remove the stitch from the left-hand needle; now insert the tip of your right-hand needle into the back of the same stitch on the left-hand needle, and purl it. Remove stitch from left hand needle.

DOUBLE-CENTERED DECREASE (S2KP)

Slip the next two stitches together, knitwise, to right-hand needle, knit the next stitch normally; now insert your left-hand needle tip into both slipped stitches, lifting them up and over the knitted stitch and off the needle, similar to the way you bind off.

capelets

keiran

PULLOVER CAPELET

SKILLS NEEDED
Stockinette Stitch
Seed Stitch
Ribbing
Increase
Change Color

SKILLS LEARNED
Knit in the Round

keiran

PULLOVER CAPELET

Finished Measurements

Neck: 8½"; across widest part: 26 ½"; across lower edge: 16"; length from center neck to center of lower edge: 12½".

Yarn

Anny Blatt Angora Super (70% angora, 30% wool; 116 yards/ 197 meters, 25 grams): medium-weight angora blend; 4 balls main color (MC), 1 ball contrast color (CC). Shown in #156 Aqua and #167 Teal.

Needles & Notions

US 8 (5 mm) 16" (40 cm) circular needle
US 8 (5 mm) 24" (60 cm) circular needle
or size needed to obtain gauge
Stitch markers, yarn needle

Gauge

14 stitches = 4" (10 cm) in Stockinette stitch (St st)

Pattern Stitches

1x1 Rib (multiple of 2 stitches; 1 round repeat)
Round 1: * K1, p1; repeat from * to end of round.
Round 2: Knit the knit stitches and purl the purl stitches as they face you.
Repeat Round 2 for 1x1 Rib.

Seed stitch (odd number of stitches; 1-round repeat)
Round 1: * K1, p1; repeat from * to last stitch, k1.
Round 2: Knit the purl stitches and purl the knit stitches as they face you.
Repeat Round 2 for Seed stitch.

Neck Band

Using the shorter circular needle and MC, CO 70 stitches; place a marker (pm) for beginning of round; join, being careful not to twist stitches. Begin 1x1 Rib; work until piece measures 2" from the beginning, or desired length for neck band..

Body

Change to St st; beginning at marker, work 1 row in St st, placing 3 additional markers as follows: k20, pm; k15, pm; k20, pm; knit remaining 15 stitches.
Shape Body: Increase 1 stitch by k1-f/b before and after each marker every other round until piece measures approximately 3½", or 1½" from collar (8 stitches increased every other round).
Change to CC; continue as established for 4 rounds, increasing every other round.
Change to MC; continue as established until piece measures 5" from the beginning (top edge of collar). Begin increasing every third round instead of every other round to slow down the flare of the capelet. Continue as established until piece measures 11" from the beginning, decreasing 1 stitch on last round, for an odd number of stitches.

Bottom Border

Change to Seed stitch and work in pattern until border measures 1½".
BO all stitches loosely in Seed stitch.
Weave in ends. Block piece to finished measurements.

KNIT IN THE ROUND

Cast on as you would for straight knitting. Make sure that your stitches all face the same way (that they aren't twisted around the needle), place marker for beginning of round.

Hold the needle with the last cast-on stitch in your right hand and the needle with the first stitch in your left hand. Insert right needle tip into first stitch on left needle, thereby joining all the stitches into a circle.

Knit around the stitches until you reach the marker, indicating that you have completed one row. Slip marker from left to right needle and continue. In circular knitting, knitting every stitch creates Stockinette stitch (no need to purl).

eloise

ONE-PIECE CAPELET

SKILLS NEEDED
Garter Stitch
Right-Slanted Decrease

SKILLS LEARNED
Yarn Over

eloise

ONE-PIECE CAPELET

Finished Measurements
See schematic

Yarn
3 balls GGH Lara (90% wool, 10% nylon; 60 yards/55 meters, 50 grams): bulky wool eyelash/faux fur; shown in #01 Black
OR
2 balls Noro Kureyon (100% wool; 110 yards/100 meters, 50 grams): medium-weight variegated wool; shown in #130 Barney's Rainbow.

Needles & Notions
US 11 (8 mm) needle or size to obtain gauge for larger capelet
OR
US 8 (5 mm) needle or size needed to obtain gauge for smaller capelet
Yarn needle, 2 to 3 yards ribbon of choice for neck

Gauge
12 sts = 4" (10 cm) in Garter stitch for larger capelet
16 sts = 4" (10 cm) in Garter stitch for smaller capelet

Pattern Stitch
Garter stitch (any number of stitches; 1 row repeat)
All rows: Knit every stitch.

Capelet
CO 120 stitches, placing a marker at 20 stitches, 40 stitches, 80 stitches, and 100 stitches; begin Garter stitch.

Shape Body: Decrease 1 stitch as follows: work to 1 stitch before marker, k2 tog; repeat from * to 1 stitch before last marker, k2tog, work to end. Work this decrease row every 3rd row 15 times (60 stitches remain).

ROW 46: K1, * yo, k2tog; repeat from * to last stitch, k1.
ROWS 47 to 50: Work in Garter stitch.
BO all stitches loosely.
Weave in ends.

Finishing
For larger capelet: do not block. Weave ribbon through holes (eyelets) at neck edge, leaving a tail on both sides for a pretty bow. For smaller capelet: lightly block to finished measurements. Make two I-cords (see page 124) and attach each to the eyelets at the front corners of the poncho. Attach pom-poms (see pages 126-127) to the ends of the I-cord. Alternatively, make one I-cord and thread each end through the corner eyelets to make a tie. Attach pom-poms to the ends.

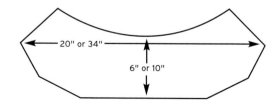

20" or 34"

6" or 10"

YARN OVER (YO)

Yarn overs make decorative increases, also known as holes. They can serve as tiny buttonholes or eyelets along a neckline, as in this pattern. They're a common feature in lace knitting.

Bring the yarn from the back to the front between the two needles.

Insert the right needle tip into next stitch, bring the yarn around to the back (on the outside, not between) and knit the next stitch.

monte

FLUTED CAPELET

SKILLS NEEDED
Stockinette Stitch

SKILLS LEARNED
Turn Work (Short Rows)

monte

FLUTED CAPELET

Finished Measurements

Bottom edge, relaxed: 26"; top edge: 19"; length: 15½"

Yarn

6 balls GGH Merino Soft (100% superwash merino wool; 184 yards/170 meters, 50 grams): fine-weight wool.
Shown in color #33 Butter.

Needles & Notions

US size 4 (3.5 mm) needle or size needed to obtain gauge
Yarn needle, stitch markers, 1½" to 2" wide satin ribbon in pale yellow, 45" long

Gauge

25 stitches = 4" (10 cm) in Stockinette stitch (St st) Each Short Row is comprised of 2 rows, a WS row and a RS row; work wrap together with wrapped stitch on next full row as follows: work to wrapped stitch, insert right-hand needle under the wrap and then into the wrapped stitch as if to knit; knit around the wrap and wrapped stitch together.

Capelet

Beginning at Front edge, CO 80 stitches; place marker after first 40 stitches for Short Row shaping.
ROW 1 (WS): Purl.
ROW 2: Knit.
ROW 3: First half of Short Row. Purl to one stitch before marker; put yarn to back (yb), slip next stitch, bring yarn to front (yf) [stitch is now wrapped]; turn work.
ROW 4: Second half of Short Row. Knit to lower edge of piece hiding wrap; Short Row completed.
ROW 5: Purl.
ROW 6: Knit.
ROWS 7 & 8: Repeat Rows 3 and 4 [Short Row].
ROW 9: Purl.
ROW 10: Knit.
ROWS 11, 13 & 15: Knit.
ROWS 12, 14 & 16: Purl.
Rows 1 through 10 create a raised section while Rows 11 through 16 create a recessed section. The wider edge of the capelet is the lower edge. Repeat Rows 1 through 16 until there are 37 raised and 36 recessed sections, ending at center Front edge.
BO all stitches loosely. Weave in ends.

Neck

CO 20 stitches.
ROW 1: Purl.
ROWS 2, 4 & 6: Knit.
ROWS 3 & 5: Purl.
ROWS 7, 9 & 11: Knit.
ROWS 8, 10 & 12: Purl.
Repeat Rows 1 through 12 until piece measures approximately 19" from the beginning, ending with Row 6.
BO all stitches loosely. Weave in ends.

Finishing

Block pieces to finished measurements.
Join Neck to Body: Pin neck section to body of capelet, stretching to match end to end. Sew neck to body.
Sew ribbon around neck, covering seam, (see tricks & techniques, opposite).

SEWING PIECES TOGETHER

Place body of capelet on a flat surface, with the upper fluted edge drawn together. Stretch neck to same width as upper body edge of capelet. Pin together and sew seam.

Place capelet on flat surface, right side up. Lay ribbon to cover seam. Pin into place. Using light colored thread, sew ribbon to capelet, covering seam.

ruby

ONE-PIECE CAPELET WITH HOOD

SKILLS NEEDED
Yarn Over
Decrease
Pick Up Stitches

SKILLS LEARNED
Read Charts

ruby

ONE PIECE CAPELET WITH HOOD

Finished Measurements

Lower edge: 74"; top: 18"; hood: 18" around base, 12½" from base to top.

Yarn

5 balls Frog Tree Alpaca Sport Weight (100% alpaca; 130 yards/120 meters, 50 grams): medium lightweight alpaca. Shown in color #23 Cherry.

Needles & Notions

US 6 (4 mm) needle or size needed to obtain gauge Stitch markers, yarn needle, T-pins for blocking, 1½" red satin ribbon OR I-cord (see page 124)and pom-poms (see page 126)

Gauge

20 stitches = 4" (10 cm) in Stockinette stitch (St st)

Shoulders

CO 88 stitches; begin Pattern stitch and shaping as follows: (see chart)

ROW 1 (RS): Knit.

ROW 2 & all even numbered rows: K4, purl to last 4 stitches, k4.

ROW 3: K4, place marker, * k2, yo, k1, yo, k1; repeat from * to last 4 stitches, place marker, k4 (128 stitches).

ROWS 5, 9, 13, 17, 21, 25, 29, 33, 37, 41, 45 & 49: Knit.

ROW 7: K4, * k2tog, [k1, yo] twice, k2tog; repeat from * to marker, k4.

ROW 11: K4, * k2tog, yo, [k1, yo] twice, k2tog; repeat from * to marker, k4 (148 stitches).

ROW 15: K4, * k2tog, yo, [k1, yo] 3 times, k2tog; repeat from * to marker, k4 (188 stitches).

ROW 19: K4, * k2tog, [k1, yo] 3 times, [k2tog] twice; repeat from * to marker, k4.

ROW 23: K4, * k2tog, yo, [k1, yo] 3 times, [k2tog] twice; repeat from * to marker, k4 (208 stitches).

ROW 27: K4, * k2tog, yo, [k1, yo] 4 times, [k2tog] twice; repeat from * to marker, k4 (248 stitches).

ROW 31: K4, * [k2tog] twice, [yo, k1] 4 times, [k2tog] twice; repeat from * to marker, k4.

ROW 35: K4, * [k2tog] twice, yo, [k1, yo] 4 times, [k2tog] twice; repeat from * to marker, k4 (268 stitches).

ROW 39: K4, * [k2tog] twice, [k1, yo] 5 times, [k2tog] twice; repeat from * to marker, k4 (288 stitches).

ROW 43: K4, * [k2tog] twice, yo, [k1, yo] 5 times, [k2tog] twice; repeat from * to marker, k4 (328 stitches).

ROW 47: K4, * [k2tog] twice, [k1, yo] 6 times, k2, [k2tog] twice; repeat from * to marker, k4 (368 stitches).

ROW 50: K4, purl to last 4 stitches, k4.

note:

Ready to tackle a chart? See pages 104-105 for the chart for this capelet as well as instructions for following a chart.

Body

ROW 51: K4, * [K2tog] 3 times, [yo, k1] 6 times, [k2tog] 3 times; repeat from * to marker, k4.

ROW 52: K4, purl to last 4 stitches, k4.

ROWS 53 to 60: Repeat Rows 51 and 52.

ROW 61: Repeat Row 51.

ROWS 62 to 66: Knit.

Repeat Rows 51 to 66 until capelet measures 13" (short) to 17" (long). BO all stitches loosely. Weave in ends.

Hood

With RS facing, beginning at right shoulder edge, pick up and knit 44 stitches, place marker for center Back, pick up and knit 44 stitches (88 stitches); turn. Purl 1 (WS) row.

Next Row (RS): [K1, p1] 4 times, * k1, yo, k2tog; repeat from * to last 4 stitches, [k1, p1] twice.

The ribbing at the beginning and end of each row creates an edge so that the hood won't curl; continue ribbing on first and last 4 stitches throughout.

Next Row: [K1, p1] twice, purl to last 4 stitches, [k1, p1] twice.
Next Row: [K1, p1] twice, knit to last 4 stitches, [k1, p1] twice.
Continue in pattern as established [4 stitches each side in ribbing; remaining stitches in St st], until hood measures 2½" from pick-up row, ending with a WS row.

Shape Hood (RS): Work to 1 stitch before marker, yo, k1, slip marker, k1, yo, work to end. Continue in pattern as established, increase 1 stitch each side of marker [by working a yo], this row, then working increases as above every 3 rows 2 times, every 4 rows 15 times (124 stitches). Continue until piece measures 12" from pick up row, ending with a WS row.

Next Row: [K1, p1] twice, k1, *yo, k2tog, k1, repeat from * to last 5 stitches, k2, p1, k1, p1.
BO all stitches in pattern.
Sew top seam. Weave in ends.

Blocking

Block piece to finished measurements as follows: Fill a basin with cool water. Dunk garment into water and gently squeeze out excess, until piece is damp but not wet. Lay piece out on a mattress or blocking board, using your T-pins to stretch it as far as you comfortably can. Place the towel over the garment and block it using your steam iron. Leave in place to dry, preferably overnight.

Ribbon or I-Cord

Thread ribbon or I-cord (see page 124) through eyelets at base of hood. Tie ribbon in bow or add pom-poms (see pages 126-127) to end of I-cord.

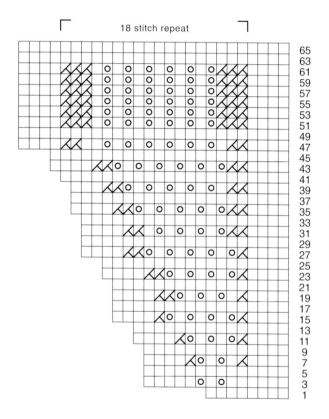

18 stitch repeat

65
63
61
59
57
55
53
51
49
47
45
43
41
39
37
35
33
31
29
27
25
23
21
19
17
15
13
11
9
7
5
3
1

KEY

☐   Knit on RS, purl on WS

◙   Yo

◪   K2tog

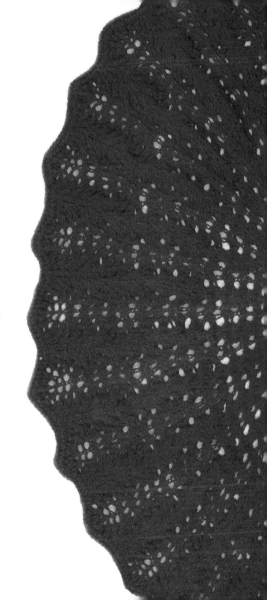

Reading Charts

Graphs are read row by row, starting at the side where the row number is seen (either right-to-left or left-to-right). Here Row 1 is read from right-to-left, then Row 2 is read from left-to-right.

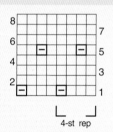

4-st rep

On some patterns, the wrong side (WS) is always purled (or knit, or worked as it appears, meaning the purl stitches are purled and the knit stitches are knit). On these charts, only the right-side (RS) rows will be depicted. For this pattern, the right-side (or odd-numbered) rows are worked in pattern. The wrong-side rows are worked as they appear (knit the knit stitches and purl the purl stitches).

Legends

Each box is a stitch. The marks in the boxes tell us which stitch to make. Here are some of the marks you might see:

KEY

☐	Knit on RS, purl on WS	C4F: Sl 2 sts to cn, hold to front, k2, k2 from cn.
⊟	Purl on RS, knit on WS	C4B: Sl 2 sts tp cn, hold to back, k2, k2 from cn.
⊙	Yo	C6B: Sl 3 sts to cn, hold to back, k3, k3 from cn.
�	K2tog	C6F: Sl 3 sts to cn, hold to front, k3, k3 from cn.
⩗	Ssk - OR - SKP	C8F: Sl 4 sts to cn, hold to front, k4, k4 from cn.
⩘	Sk2p: Slip 1, k2tog, PSSO	C8B: Sl 4 sts to cn, hold to back, k4, k4 from cn.
⧄	Twisted st: k1-tbl	
⧅	Make 1	FCp: Sl 1 st to cn, hold to front, p1, k1 from cn.
⫽	Double centered dec	BCp: Sl 1 st to cn, hold to back, k1, p1 from cn.
▨	No stitch	
●	Bobble	
∨	Slip 1	
⊬	Inc-R	
⊐	Inc-L	

eudora

CARDIGAN CAPELET

SKILLS NEEDED
Stockinette Stitch
Garter Stitch
Knit Increase
Change Colors
Right- and Left-Slanting Decreases

eudora

CARDIGAN CAPELET

Finished Measurements

Neck: 26"; lower edge: 55"; length: 16½"

Yarn

1 skein each in 3 colors Tahki Donegal Tweed
(100% pure new wool; 183 yards/169 meters, 100
grams): medium-weight wool. Shown in colors
A) Meadow Green (color 892)
B) Autumn Orange (color 893)
C) Charcoal (color 895)

Needles & Notions

US 9 (5.5 mm) 24" or 36" (60 or 90 cm) circular needle
or size needed to obtain gauge
Stitch markers, yarn needle, Scandinavian Frog Closure

Gauge

17 stitches = 4" (10 cm) in Stockinette Stitch (St st)

Abbreviations

K1-f/b: Knit increase (knit through the front and back of
the stitch)
Ssk: Slip, slip, knot (see tricks & techniques, page 59)

Capelet

Using color A, CO 236 stitches for lower edge. Work in Garter stitch for the first 3 rows
(bottom border), placing markers after first 3 stitches and before last 3 stitches.

ROWS 1, 3 & 5: K3, * k2tog, k8, [k1-f/b] twice, k9, ssk; repeat from * to marker, k3

ROWS 2 & 4: K3, purl to marker, k3.

ROWS 6 to 8: Knit.

ROW 9: K3, *k2tog, k8, k1-f/b, k10, ssk, k2tog, k8, [k1-f/b] twice, k9, ssk; repeat from *
to last marker, k3 (231 stitches remain).

ROWS 10 & 12: K3, purl to marker, k3.

ROWS 11 & 13: K3, * k2tog, k8, [k1-f/b] twice, k8, ssk, k2tog, k8, [k1-f/b] twice, k9, ssk;
repeat from * to marker, k3.

ROWS 14 to 16: Knit.

ROW 17: K3, * k2tog, k8, [k1-f/b] twice, k8, ssk, k2tog, k8, k1-f/b, k10, ssk; repeat from
* to marker, k3 (226 stitches remain).

ROWS 18 & 20: K3, purl to marker, k3.

ROWS 19 & 21: K3, * k2tog, k8, [k1-f/b] twice, k8, ssk; repeat from * to marker, k3.

ROWS 22 to 24: Knit.

ROW 25: Change to color B; k3, * k2tog, k8, [k1-f/b] twice, k6, [ssk] twice, k2tog, k8,
[k1-f/b] twice, k8, ssk; repeat from * to marker, k3 (221 stitches remain).

ROWS 26 & 28: K3, purl to marker, k3.

ROWS 27 & 29: K3, * k2tog, k8, [k1-f/b] twice, k7, ssk, k2tog, k8, [k1-f/b] twice, k8,
ssk; repeat from * to marker, k3.

ROWS 30 to 32: Knit.

ROW 33: K3, * k2tog, k8, [k1-f/b] twice, k7, ssk, k2tog, k8, [k1-f/b] twice, k6, [ssk]
twice; repeat from * to marker, k3 (216 stitches remain).

ROWS 34 & 36: K3, purl to marker, k3.

ROWS 35 & 37: K3, *k2tog, k8, [k1-f/b] twice, k7, ssk; repeat from * to marker, k3.

ROWS 38 to 40: Knit.

ROW 41: K3, * [k1-f/b] twice, k6, [k1-f/b] twice, k7, ssk, k2tog, k8, [k1-f/b] twice, k7, ssk; repeat from * to marker, k3 (211 stitches remain).

ROWS 42 & 44: K3, purl to marker, k3.

ROWS 43 & 45: K3, * k2tog, k7, [k1-f/b] twice, k7, ssk, k2tog, k8, [k1-f/b] twice, k7, ssk; repeat from * to marker, k3.

ROWS 46 to 48: Knit.

ROW 49: K3, * k2tog, k7, [k1-f/b] twice, k7, ssk, k2tog, k2tog, k6, [k1-f/b] twice, k7, ssk; repeat from * to marker, k3 (206 stitches remain).

ROWS 50 & 52: K3, purl to marker, k3.

ROW 51: K3, * k2tog, k7, [k1-f/b] twice, k7, ssk; rep from * to marker, k3.

ROW 53: Change to color C; k3, * k2tog, k7, [k1-f/b] twice, k7, ssk; repeat from * to marker, k3.

ROWS 54 to 56: Knit.

ROW 57: K3, * k2tog, k7, [k1-f/b] twice, k5, [ssk] twice, k2tog, k7, [k1-f/b] twice, k7, ssk; repeat from * to marker, k3 (201 stitches remain).

ROWS 58 & 60: K3, purl to marker, k3.

ROW 59: K3 * k2tog, k7, [k1-f/b] twice, k6, ssk, k2tog, k7, [k1-f/b] twice, k5, [ssk] twice; repeat from * to marker, k3 (196 stitches remain).

ROW 61: K3, * [k2tog] twice, k5, [k1-f/b] twice, k6, ssk, k2tog, k7, [k1-f/b] twice, k6, ssk; repeat from * to marker, k3 (191 stitches remain).

ROWS 62 to 64: Knit.

ROW 65: K3, * k2tog, k6, [k1-f/b] twice, k6, ssk, [k2tog] twice k5, [k1-f/b] twice, k6, ssk; repeat from * to marker, k3 (186 stitches remain).

ROWS 66 & 68: K3, purl to marker, k3.

ROW 67: K3, * k2tog, k6, [k1-f/b] twice, k6, ssk, k2tog, k6, [k1-f/b] twice, k4, [ssk] twice; repeat from * to marker, k3 (181 stitches remain).

ROW 69: K3, *k2tog, k6, [k1-f/b] twice, k5, ssk, k2tog, k6, [k1-f/b] twice, k4, [ssk] twice; repeat from * to marker, k3 (176 stitches remain).

ROWS 70 to 72: Knit.

ROW 73: K3, * [k2tog] twice, k4, [k1-f/b] twice, k3, [ssk] twice; repeat from * to marker, k3 (156 stitches remain).

ROWS 74 & 76: K3, purl to marker, k3.

ROW 75: K3, * [k2tog] twice, k3, [k1-f/b] twice, k2, [ssk] twice; repeat from * to marker, k3 (136 stitches remain).

ROW 77: K3, * [k2tog] twice, k2, [k1-f/b] twice, k1, [ssk] twice; repeat from * to marker, k3 (116 stitches remain).

ROWS 78 to 80: Knit.

ROW 81: K3, * [k2tog] twice, k1, [k1-f/b] twice, [ssk] twice; repeat from * to marker, k3 (96 stitches remain).

ROW 82: K3, purl to marker, k3.

Neck Band

ROWS 83 & 85: K4, * p3, k1; repeat from * to last 4 stitches, p1, k3.

ROW 84: K4, * p1, k3; repeat from * to end.

ROW 86: K4, * p1, k2tog, k1, p1, k3; rep from * to last 4 stitches, p1, k3.

ROW 87: K4, * p3, k1, p2, k1; repeat from * to last 4 stitches, p1, k3.

ROW 88: K4, * p1, k2, p1, k3; repeat from * to last 4 stitches, p1, k3.

ROW 89: K4, * p2tog, k1, p2, k1; repeat from * to last 4 stitches, p1, k3.

ROW 90: K4, * p1, k2; repeat from * to last 4 stitches, p1, k3.

BO all stitches loosely. Weave in ends.

Finishing

Block piece to finished measurements, being careful not to flatten texture. Sew hook and eye halves of frog to each corner of neck band.

extras

duchess

PUPPY PONCHO

SKILLS NEEDED
Knit and Purl

SKILLS LEARNED
Make One Increase
Ribbing

duchess

PUPPY PONCHO

Finished Measurements

See "Measuring Your Dog"

Yarn

3 balls Anny Blatt Rustique (100% pure wool; 64 yards/
59 meters, 50 grams): machine washable, medium-weight
(#4) wool. Shown in color #341650 Tzigane (bright
variegated yarn).

Needles & Notions

US 10 (6 mm) needles or size needed to obtain gauge
Stitch marker, yarn needle, measuring tape

Gauge

16 stitches = 4" (10 cm) in Stockinette stitch

Abbreviations

M1 (increase): Make one (see *tricks & techniques*,
opposite)
K1-f/b (increase): knit through the front and back of
the stitch

Pattern Stitch

1x1 Rib (multiple of 2 stitches; 1 row repeat)
Row 1: *K1, p1; repeat from * across.
Repeat Row 1 for 1x1 Rib.

Measuring Your Dog

Measure your dog from collar (neck) down chest to beginning of legs for measurement
"A." Then measure around the back from top of one leg to the top of the other leg for
measurement "B."

Front (chest) Panel

CO on 22 stitches; begin 1x1 Rib. Continue in pattern for 2 rows.
Shape Front Panel: Continuing in 1x1 Rib as established, increase 1 stitch at both ends of
every row as follows: P1, M1, work in rib to last stitch, M1, k1.
Working increased stitches in rib as they become established, continue shaping until
panel measures "A." BO all stitches in rib. Weave in ends.

Back Panel

CO 54 stitches, placing marker after 27th stitch; begin 1x1 rib.
Continue in pattern for 2 rows, ending with a WS row. Change to Stockinette stitch (St st).
Shape Back Panel: (RS) * K1, M1, knit to marker; k1-f/b one stitch before and one stitch
after marker; knit to last stitch, M1, k1. Purl 1 row even. Repeat from *, increasing 4
stitches every other row, until piece measures "B." ending with a WS row.
(RS) Change to 1x1 rib; Work in rib to marker; turn, leaving remaining stitches unworked.
Working on these stitches only, work the next 3 rows in pattern.
BO all stitches in rib. Join yarn to remaining stitches [opposite side of marker], ready to
work a RS row. Work as for first side. Weave in ends.

Finishing

Block pieces to measurements "A" and "B," being careful not to flatten rib.
Sew Front panel to Back panel.

MAKE ONE (M1)

Left-slanting increase:
Insert tip of left-hand
needle from front to back
into the horizontal strand
between the stitch just
worked and the next stitch.

Knit this stitch through
the back loop (this twists
the stitch to prevent
a hole).

sizing

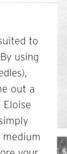

We're all different: a little bigger here, a little smaller there. One of the benefits of the poncho is its flexibility where size is concerned—most ponchos fit most people. But some of us are chestier than others or have broader shoulders; some of us are petite—and some of us have kids! What if we want to make a poncho for our twelve-year-old daughter? Here are some tricks you can use to easily customize the size of a poncho.

Changing Your Needles and Yarn

This is the easiest way of tweaking a garment's size. Undoubtedly, there's a host of folks who'll poo-poo this method, but with a little know-how we think it works just fine.

Each pattern uses yarn and needles suited to create that poncho in a specific size. By using a yarn that's thinner (and thinner needles), you can easily adjust a pattern to come out a step smaller. We've done this in both Eloise (page 94) and Ginger (page 62). By simply using a lightweight yarn instead of a medium weight yarn, your gauge —and therefore your garment—will come out smaller.

But do keep the texture in mind. Take the time to really understand the nature of the original yarn used so that you can substitute accurately. Was the original pattern knit in a bulky mohair? A medium-weight cotton won't

achieve the same look, and the drape will be drastically different. Staying within fiber type is a safe bet.

Naturally this type of sizing works both ways—up and down. And when in doubt, run your choices by the staff of the knitting shop where you buy your yarn. Ask them for recommendations and also for their opinion of your substitute yarn choice.

Many of you have figured out by now that knitting uses math—a lot. This technique does too, so be warned.

When your poncho is made of a repeating pattern (such as Ruby, page 102), many times you can simply add or remove one of the repetitions to tweak the size. Using Ruby as our example, we see that the pattern starts with a repetition of 4 stitches. There are 22 repetitions, resulting in a cast-on of 88 stitches.

To tweak the pattern and make it smaller, do 21 repetitions instead of 22 (multipy 4 x 21 and you'll come up with a cast-on of 84 stitches). The chart will still work just fine, just remember that the stitch count will be different as you go and you'll have to make adjustments when you add on the hood.

You'll notice that the patterns in this book have finished measurements. Use your measuring tape to determine if those measurements are right for you, allowing for ease—you don't want a skin-tight poncho! To tweak for adult sizes a touch bigger or smaller, go up or down one yarn weight (see CYCA chart, page 17). To shrink for tweens, you'll want to bump down a couple of weights. Sometimes this isn't possible, for example if the pattern was written using lightweight yarn you can't bump down two weights. In this case, try re-working the pattern using increments and measurements. If the pattern uses an 18-stitch repeat 20 times, try using the 18-stitch repeat 18 or 19 times instead. If you feel uncomfortable with this process, go to the shop where you bought your yarn for advice. The folks there can help you either by re-working it or getting you in touch with a knitting specialist in the area who can re-work it for you. (Or better yet, teach you how to do it yourself!)

add-ons

Hoods

There's no hard-and-fast rule on how a hood is made. Our version is very simple and easily customized. The math may seem daunting at first, but it's not too hard when taken step-by-step. Here's how:

First, decide if you want an opening (or space) at the front base (neckline) of your hood. In other words, will the hood come up from the sides or completely surround your face? Most will come up from the sides, so depending on your gauge, choose the amount of stitches that give you a space of a couple of inches at the base of the hood. Pick up the stitches around the base, placing a marker at the halfway point.

You'll want to add some inches for ease, usually about 30 percent. How to figure that out? Measure the circumference of the neck, then multiply the neck length by 30 percent. That will be your ease in inches. Now multiply that amount by your gauge and you'll know how many to stitches to increase.

Add the ease amount to the length of the neck and you'll get the total finished length at the top. Divide this number in half to find the height of your hood. Space your increases evenly through the hood height to add the ease.

A self-finished hood has a border around the face so it won't curl. Alternatively you could sew back the edge to make a tube through which to thread a drawstring (I-cord or a crochet chain). Never use a drawstring around the neck or face of a child's poncho—it's not safe. That's why we use the self-finishing model in our ponchos.

Cowl Necks

We're fans of the cowl neck and have used variations on that theme in Carson (page 30), Eleanor (page 34), and Greta (page 38). Adding a cowl neck is easy. If you're knitting in the round, start at the top of the poncho and add on a few inches worth of stitches, knitting in the round and decreasing as you go until you reach the poncho neckline. Continue to knit your poncho as directed from there. Keep in mind that the cowl gets turned out, so if you want the stitches to match, knit them in reverse for the neck. Adding a cowl neck once the poncho is made is easy breezy! Just pick up the stitches around the neck and either join and increase, for a cowl-y turtleneck effect, or turn, for a split cowl à la Carson.

I-Cord

Using double-pointed needles, cast on three stitches (fewer for thinner I-cord, more for thicker I-cord). Knit those three stitches, but do not turn the work. Instead, slide those three stitches to the other end of the dpn. Knit those stitches, bringing the yarn across and knitting them normally. Repeat, sliding the stitches every row until your cord is desired length. Bind off.

We tied the I-cord through each of the corners of this child's capelet then attached the pom-poms.

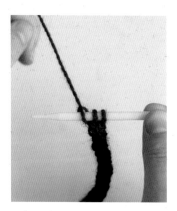

Fringe

Our Desirée pattern features a pictorial on how to attach fringe (page 49). There, we use two strands held together and spaced out every couple of stitches. That doesn't mean you have to do the same. Experiment with your fringe: cluster single strands very closely together for a lush look; use five to ten strands at a time for tassels; or make your fringe extra long—or extra short—for added drama.

Pom-Poms

Perhaps you've tried to make pom-poms using cardboard circles.

Perhaps, like us, this gave you a headache.

Go out and get yourself a pom-pom maker

and some sharp embroidery scissors.

They don't cost much and they make life a lot more fun.

Here's how it works:

1. Put the two pieces together like so
2. Wrap the yarn around the pieces, using lots of yarn for a thick, luscious pom-pom
   Repeat Steps 1 and 2 with the other half of the pom-pom maker
3. Click the two halves of the pom-pom maker together
4. With very sharp scissors cut around the pom-pom between the two halves
5. Tie yarn tightly around the pom-pom center
6. Carefully remove pom-pom maker parts
7. Trim unruly bits for a clean look
8. So festive!

resources *KITS AVAILABLE AT VIVAPONCHO.COM*

Article Pract

5010 Telegraph Avenue
Oakland, California 94609
Tel. (510) 652-7435
www.articlepract.com

Yarn Distributors

Anny Blatt

7796 Boardwalk
Brighton, Michigan 48116
Toll Free: (800) 531-9276
www.annyblatt.com

Blue Sky Alpacas

P. O. Box 387
St. Francis, Minnesota 55070
Toll Free: (888) 460-8862
www.blueskyalpacas.com

Brown Sheep Yarns

100662 County Road 16
Mitchell, Nebraska 69357
Toll Free: (800) 826-9136
www.brownsheep.com

Cascade Yarns

P.O. Box 58168
Tukwila, WA 98138
Toll Free: (800) 548-1048
www.cascadeyarns.com

Colinette

28 North Bacton Hill Road
Malvern, Pennsylvania 19355
Toll Free: (800) 252-3934
www.colinette.com

Crystal Palace Yarns

160 23rd Street
Richmond, California 94804
Tel. (510) 237-9988
www.crystalpalaceyarns.com
www.straw.com

Lana Grossa

1338 Ross Street
Petaluma, California 94954
Toll Free: (800) 289-9276
www.lanagrossa.com

Frog Tree Alpaca

T + C Imports
P.O. Box 1119
East Dennis, Massachusetts 02641

GGH

1323 Scott Street
Petaluma, California 94954
Toll Free: (800) 733-9276
www.muenchyarns.com

Rowan

4 Townsend West Unit 8
Nashua, NH 03063
Toll Free: (800) 445-9276
www.knitrowan.com

Tahki Yarns

70-30 80th Street, Building 36
Ridgewood, New York 11385
Toll Free: (800) 338-9276
www.tahkistacycharles.com

Tess Designer Yarns

33 Strawberry Point
Steuben, Maine 04680
Toll Free: (800) 321-8377
www.tessdesigneryarns.com

Scandinavian Frog Closure: Aurora Yarns

850 Airport Street, Unit 3A
Moss Beach, CA 94038
Tel. (650) 728-2730

recommended reading

All-Purpose Knitting Books

The books on this list are general, all-purpose knitting books, plus some specialized books that we think are fabulous. The answer to any question you might have can be found in at least one of these books.

Vogue Knitting: Ultimate Knitting, Vogue Knitting Editors (Sterling Publishing Co., Inc.)

Stitch 'n Bitch: The Knitter's Handbook, Debbie Stoller (Workman Publishing)

Mary Thomas' Knitting Book, Mary Thomas (Dover Publications)

The Knitting Experience: The Knit Stitch, Sally Melville (XRX Books)

Knitting in Plain English, Maggie Righetti (St. Martin's Press)

Nicky Epstein's Knitted Embellishments, Nicky Epstein (Interweave Press, Inc.)

A First Treasury of Knitting Patterns, Barbara Walker (Schoolhouse Press)

A Second Treasury of Knitting Patterns, Barbara Walker (Schoolhouse Press)

Anything by Elizabeth Zimmermann

Our Favorite Knitting Books

There are so many amazing books out there, we couldn't possibly list them all. So here's a list of some of the books we're in love with right now.

Weekend Knitting, Melanie Falick (Stewart, Tabori & Chang)

Stitch 'n Bitch Nation (featuring a handbag pattern by Leslie Barbazette!), Debbie Stoller (Workman Publishing)

Kids Knitting: Projects for Kids of All Ages, Melanie Falick (Artisan Publishers)

Last Minute Knitted Gifts, Joelle Hoverson (Stewart, Tabori & Chang)

Scarf Style, Pam Allen (Interweave Press)

The Yarn Girls' Guide to Simple Knits, Julie Carles and Jordana Jacobs (Clarkson Potter)

Rowan Junior, Kim Hargreaves (Rowan Yarns, Ltd.)

A Season's Tale, Kim Hargreaves (Rowan Yarns, Ltd.)

Felted Knits, Bev Galeskas (Interweave Press)

Comforts of Home, Erika Knight (Martingale & Company)

Norsk Strikkedesign: A Collection from Norway's Foremost Knitting Designers (Unicorn Books & Crafts, Inc.)

Knit Scarves!, Candi Jensen (Workman Publishing)

Kaffe Fassett's Pattern Library, Kaffe Fassett (Taunton Press)

Toy Knits, Debbie Bliss (St. Martin's Press)

Websites

These websites have free knitting patterns and are rad!

www.knitty.com

www.magknits.com (featuring Frida from this book)

We Read These Periodicals

Rebecca Magazine (www.rebecca-online.com)
Rowan Magazine (www.knitrowan.com)
Interweave Knits (www.interweave.com/knit)
R2 (www.knitr2.com)
Vogue Knitting (vogueknitting.com)

index